Seasons of Her Soul

Tamara O'Leary

BookLeaf Publishing

Presentation by *BookLeaf Publishing*

Web: www.bookleafpub.com

E-mail: info@bookleafpub.com

ISBN: 9789357692083

First edition 2022

DEDICATION

To all who are hurting and hoping for healing.
To all who are struggling with their thoughts,
feelings, emotions and mental health.

You are not alone.

I see you.

ACKNOWLEDGEMENT

BookLeaf Publishing www.bookleafpub.com

Instagram

Ernest Hemingway - "We are all broken. That's how the light gets in"

A few close friends - You know who you are ♡

PREFACE

This little book (my first!) is actually such a gift.
An insightful gift, that holds so much more
meaning for me than you will ever truly know.
It's an exposure of the rawest places in my heart
and the deepest depths of my soul.
It's a breaking open and a pouring out.
A real-life snapshot of my personal journey with
mental illness and mental wellness.
And it's my absolute honor, to have this
incredible opportunity to share my soul with
you!
Thank you for reading 🖤

MENTALLY DROWNING

She cried her heart out in the shower this
morning
Desperate, anguishing tears
Uncontrollable, convulsing sobs

Anxiety within was strangling her
Clenching and crippling
Incarcerating her into a frozen-like state

All the while
No one heard her cries
No one shared her suffering

No one knew how defeated she felt
How crumpled her courage was
How convoluted her coping skills had become
How much it was consuming her

Porcelain contours cradled her body as she
wailed
Powerlessly
Fearfully
and

Alone

QUICKSAND

Damn, this heart on my sleeve
Causes trouble with you every time
I get sucked in deep
Familiar tears, I weep
No matter how many times I try

This time, I'll dodge the sinkhole
Knowing full well, that's not who I am
Further and further, I go
Till you you've swallowed me whole
Drowning me in emotional quicksand

THROWN TO THE WOLVES

Throw me to the wolves
Can't you see, they are ravenous!
Appease their hungry-eyed stare
With another hasty, careless devour

Don't wait for them to salivate
Nor stalk with pensive-like approach
Just let them pounce
And wield their familiar, ferocious snarl

My weakness is insatiable
A mere morsel for their gluttony
I fall prey time and time again
And defenseless, I succumb

THE ME THAT I BECOME

Dreading another day's arrival
That fiercely, familiar response engulfs me
Stirring pent-up emotions
Festering unhealed hurts
Reawakening forlorn feelings that had been laid
to rest

Jealousy swarms
Passive-aggressive thoughts clamor and clang
Selfish pride begins to rear her not so pretty
head
I fight the urge to lash out
Drawing into this unpleasant pattern
I am lured into a version of me that I am not
proud of
A version that is unkind and unladylike
Ill-natured, snidely and spiteful
A me that begrudges being second in command
A me that I don't want to become
A me that I want gone

WE ALL BLEED RED

We all hurt
And we all heal
Some parts we share and some parts we conceal

Some we get over
Some are more than we can bear
Some leave us with the heaviest hearts in despair

Cracks and crevices precede our brokenness
Parting the pieces just enough
Slivers of light emit and illuminate
Like shiny diamonds in the rough

When the light inside glows brighter
In time, our hurts and heartaches mend
Gaining insight from experience
Finding new ways to love again

It's true, we all bleed red
But our healing palettes are one-of-a-kind
Prepared to paint in living colour
The canvas of body, heart and mind

WARMTH OF THE SUN

Eyes closed
Deep in slumber
A sudden sound breaks the silence
I feel the steady beat of my heart's rhythm
Awakening my senses
And rousing my reverie

Eyes open
Alert to my surroundings
A soft light peers through my slatted blinds
A hazy reminder that a new day has begun
I step outside

A gentle breeze
Spreads the scent
Freshly cut grass, sprinkled with dew
Over the horizon
Beauty spreads its wings
Gratefully, a peace settles in my soul
Awaiting the warmth of the sun

Magnificent rays
Full of hope and promise
Warming hearts, allaying fears
Easing uncertainties, drying tears

Even from behind the clouds my healing begins
A therapy all of its own

Hours pass
Evening approaches
Daylight begins to fade
Revealing with it a crimson sky
Making way for moon and stars
And the darkness that prevails

All around me
Graces abound
Unwavering like God's mercies
So too, the sun will shine
Fresh and new each morning
Dazzling us with its brilliance
Unveiling its warmth
Remedying both mind and body

Contentedly,
Blanketing my face
A smile forms
I close my eyes

FINDING TREASURE

I hope when my son is my age
He has built upon the values and morals I've
tried to teach and instill in him, and has a strong
sense of faith and purpose as he grows and
matures into manhood

I hope when my son is my age
He has learned some valuable lessons from the
choices he's made, and is comfortable with the
consequences of those choices

I hope when my son is my age
He has established himself in a career that he
loves, and it reaps joy, satisfaction and a sense of
accomplishment

I hope when my son is my age
He has been given the chance to experience and
cherish the gift of a loyal and loving spouse, and
that their union is blessed with a love that is
mutual, understanding and unconditional

I hope when my son is my age
He has the miraculous privilege of becoming a
parent, is able to experience the awe and wonder

of a child's love, and feels the same sense of
pride as I do right now watching him grow

I hope when my son is my age
He realizes that age, in itself, is just a number,
and that the real valuables in life, are the
treasures we find along the way

GAME FACE

Parked at the side of the road
She cries the same salty, sad tears that she cried
yesterday
And the day before that
Seems to be the norm lately
These woes taking a toll on her health

The last year has been a trying one, much in part
due to circumstances beyond her control
Injury has affected her capabilities and dwindled
her confidence
Alliances with key colleagues have become
tense
Communication has become strained,
misunderstood, or overlooked
And that makes her sad
Because going from spending the last 10 years
in a job she loves, to counting down the minutes
of every 9 to 5
Is not who she is
But somehow, her work no longer exudes the
passion and pride that it used to
The struggle to find joy in each day adds even
more weight to the heavy sadness she's already
carrying

And if she were to be honest
She's not sure how much more she can take
Or how much longer she can wear this game
face

DARK CLOUD

I feel like I'm starting to fall
Back into that place again
The place that I try hard to hide from
The place I dislike being in

That dark cloud that comes out of nowhere
Makes happiness so hard to discern
I'm not sure of the why or the how
I just sense that familiar return

The grief that follows is familiar
Both unwelcome and heavy on my heart
No idea of the cause or circumstance
Or how to make it depart

My challenge is healthy coping skills
Thoughts, feelings and actions I need to peruse
Most importantly, I need to remember
That the only way out is through

So, if all I can manage is self-care
And the perseverance to muddle my way
Today's gloom can't last forever, when
Tomorrow's gift is a brand new day

PIECES

To the outside world, she's just a regular gal
An easy smile, outgoing personality, and an
ever-friendly disposition
But she sees none of that

She sees someone cowardly and inferior
Powerless, not-good-enough, and a failure
Simple tasks are overwhelming
She feels numb and can barely function

There is no smile
Her soul is scarred and her heart, battered and
bruised
She feels so empty inside
A vacancy so deep and so dark

She can't swallow her sadness anymore
She knows she can't possibly bear another day,
hurting this way
The pain is unbearable
It's squeezing the life right out of her
She's trapped, and there's no escape

Shamefully, she wallows
Sorrow and self-pity are her best friends

How did she get to this place?
Tears fall from her dark eyes
She's not exactly sure for which reason this time,
but they do
Blurring her vision
Drowning her

She stumbles
She crumbles
Her fragile heart shatters into a million little
pieces
Her soul follows, and those pieces fall too
No one hears a sound
No one feels her pain
No one hears her cry
Or dries her tears
She can't hold on
And she can't let go
So, in the end
All that remains
Are the pieces left behind

MORNING MERCIES

A welcome breeze
Filters through the evergreens
Lofty boughs, swaying freely back and forth
Perpetual ripples
Lap gently along the water's edge
Lulling sleepy mallards as they nestle in the tall
grass

Solemnly, I sit
On a wrought iron bench
Staring at my reflection in the water
I feel defenseless and defeated
And the weight of my sagging spirit
Is almost too hard to bear

As nightfall nears
The lake begins to twinkle under the decending
sun
All at once, my wallowing is interrupted
"The sun will rise and a new day will come"

Timely words
A bedtime mantra as I lay my weary head
And a prayer for hopeful healing
By morning light

THERAPY STROLL

Between the fields of corn, they walked
Beneath bright sun and clear blue sky
Like many times before, they talked
Of their hardships, hurts, or days gone by

Similar circumstance, and mutual understanding
Indeed, their worlds were like two parallel lines
The stroll was therapeutic, a well-timed blessing
An airing out of both hearts and minds

At times in life, you need a friend
And not just any old friend will do
It's the cherished ones, on whom you can depend
That are forever trusted, tried and true

CORNFIELD SUNSET

On comfy, pillowed couches
They sat watching the setting sun
Spreading its blanket over meadows of greens
and golds

Beyond the cornfield
Pastel hues emerged into radient pinks and
purples
Signaling the end of another beautiful summer's
day

Two forever friends
Immerse themselves in timely, familiar
comraderie
Work, health, life, family
Similar stories, stresses and worries
Catching up like old times
'Til the early hours of morn

Surrounded by a cornfield sunset
A backdrop of crickets
Waterfall trickles
And a healing space for two hearts and two
minds

HER ANGELS and HER ANGELS 2

On this, the day she went away
The 23rd of December
My mind is full of thoughts of you
That sad news, I still remember

Her parting gave no warning
And you were so very young
How suddenly she left this world
When that song, her Angels sung

Much younger then, so too was I
But I tried my very best
The only thing I thought might help
Was hold you tightly to my chest

I wanted to be there for you
To somehow ease your pain
Those early years have come and gone
But today, I feel the same

If I could, I'd wipe all the tears
You've shed along the way
I'd hug you tight, though from afar
In a warm, comforting embrace

Her memory lives inside of you
In that way, you'll never be apart
And still, she watches over you
From break of day until dark

She sees your every struggle
Every challenge, every fear
She feels the ache you're feeling
And she hears your every prayer

I know she's up there beaming
At the man that you've become
I'm sure she's very proud of you
Her precious, youngest son

And though your heart is hurting
She wants you to live on
My hope is that this little poem
Helps you endure and carry on

And if you need to be reminded
Just look up to heaven above
Her Angels, they will comfort you
And surround you with Her love

HER ANGELS 2

On a winter's day, she was called away
Twas the 7th of December
Blanketed both in sorrow and grace
A day you always will remember

Though her parting heeded warning
Her final moments, they still stung
When peacefully she left this world
And her song, her Angels sung

Such a loving, remarkable woman
She touched the lives of many
Her devotion, strength and empathy
Awarded her a lifelong legacy

She bestowed a rare compassion
It truly was one of her many gifts
Her steady, selfless, caring nature
Never failed or waned a bit

I know you miss her everyday
Life now, is not the same
On earth, she may have come and gone
But in your heart, she still remains

For inside of you, her memory lives
Just like from the very start

And now, she watches over you
From daybreak until dark

She sees your every struggle
Every challenge, every fear
She feels the ache you're feeling
And she hears your every prayer

I'm sure she's up there beaming
At the beings you've all become
I know she's very proud of you
Her two daughters and her son

And though your heart is hurting
She wants you to live on
My hope is that this little poem
Helps you endure and carry on

So, if you need to be reminded
Just look up to heaven above
Her Angels, they will comfort you
And surround you with Her love

TAILSPIN

I was sent in a flutter
With the words you had uttered
An unexpected shock that caught me off guard

Like a solid sucker punch
Straight and square into my guts
The breath froze inside of my lungs with its
force

I was too stunned to know what to say
We have heart-to-heart talks nearly everyday
Was there some sort of turn of events that I
missed?

Loaded feelings erupted and began spinning
Negative thoughts started winning
My heart pounded into a tailspin flying right out
of my chest

Was this about me or about us?
This wasn't something that we discussed!
My first thoughts came rushing forth to the
rescue

Torrential tears steadily flowing

Insecurities and fears growing
With my hearstrings clutched tight
I held my tongue

BLINK OF AN EYE

It's so easy to be mindlessly unaware
Of all the things we are given
Without even having to ask
The gift of another day
And another day after that
Almost frivolously, we take for granted that
another one will always come
But, have you ever stopped to wonder
Just how much of a privilege 'another day' is?
To know that you have another chance
Another try
Another opportunity
To be better, do better, or live better than you
were the day before
Such a blessing
And sadly, sometimes, it's not until you see how
quickly it can be taken away
That we appreciate life itself
Every day is such a precious gift
May we be mindful and grateful for that
privilege
Cherish every sunrise and sunset
Knowing that any instant
It can be gone in the blink of an eye

ON THE OTHER SIDE

They say
Without struggle, there is no strength
Without pain, there is no gain
Without mistakes, there are no lessons
The hardest part is in the meantime
That space between now and then, before and
after
The place where our faith is tested, time and
time again
In this life, there will be hardships
We must endure heartache, stress and strain
And though it may feel like we will never get
there, we have to keep going
And we have to somehow trust that once we turn
the corner, there must be something better
waiting for us on the other side

ROAD TRIP

Your path toward healing has begun
Brave steps taken, one by one
With progress made in every day
And lessons learned along the way

This healing journey is no small feat
It's emotional work in the driver's seat
Reconstruct, repair and self-care to embrace
On this bumpy joyride, there is no race

Pot holes, gravel, twists and turns
Uncharted routes to discover and learn
Roadblocks, curves and detour signs
Fractured fragments, paved smooth with time

For with every part of your rebuild
New trades are acquired, along with skills
Courage and confidence will direct your steer
And those roadmap worries will disappear

Focus face-forward on your windshield view
And leave what's behind in that rear mirror view
Our healing highways are all unique
And no one speeds down easy street

BRAVE BEGINNINGS

Brave, beautiful girl
A New Year has emerged
A fresh, clean slate
Perfect for growth and new beginnings
You struggled
You persevered
You overcame
You conquered
A restoration of health and healing awaits, but
fear not!
Everything you need is already inside of you
You are strong and courageous
You are capable
You are resilient
And you are not alone
Every challenge you face, you willl confront
And your struggles will turn into strength
Remember this when your faith falters or your
willfulness wanes
You can do this. Be patient. Persevere
One more minute
One more hour
One more day
And then repeat
Keep taking those sturdy strides

Don't worry if you backtrack, or if you retrace
your steps a hundred times
Make it part of the dance!
Forward is forward, no matter the speed
Or how tiny the steps

SOUTHLINE SERENADE
(BILLY'S SONG)

You had the heart of purest gold
An infectious laugh and grin
Made everyone feel at ease
In any room that you walked in

Strong values and country roots
A hard day's work, you had no fear
You took great pride in the family farm
Tending the seasons labour year to year

Your talents and virtues were many
So hard to just name a few
Kind, generous, clever, charismatic
Such a blessing to all you knew

My earliest, fondest memories
Had you entertaining us from a young age
Swaying, steadily, to and fro
In front of the Siegner home fireplace

Donning yellow-footed, onesie pajamas
Steely blue eyes, focused and sincere
A stance of fierce determination
You stood proudly, singing for all to hear

Kenny Rodgers was your childhood idol
'Lucille' and 'The Gambler', I remember most
Of late, Luke Combs became fan favourite
'Hurricane' and 'When it Rains It Pours'

When we had the chance to be together
We all loved to gather 'round
You played and sang your heart out
Passion penetrated every sound

That sad day came without warning
It seemed God had other plans for you
There would be no last strum of your guitar
No last song to bid adieu

At the first sound of lyrics or a melody
Your presence comes alive in my mind
Tears fall away and an angel whispers
A serenade over the fields of the Southline

LETTING GO LIKE NOVEMBER

Mid-October's ripened leaves
Reluctantly, flutter and fall
Wither and wilt in morning's frost
A surrender to the season's call

Some cling tightly to their branches
Afraid and ill-prepared to say goodbye
Still, layer upon layer, they collect and clutter
Much like those doubts heap in her mind

Perhaps this state of transformation
And adaptation of tumbling leaves
Is a call for self-discovery, of faith
Or affirmation of self-belief

What is tethered to her thoughts?
Have expectations gone unmet?
Are there fragments of unworthiness?
Comparison? Belittlement?

Mother Nature heeds her perfect timing
Signaling autumn's graceful end
Routine, perpetual and old-fashioned
Winter's wonderland soon begins

She too, must allow herself some space
To sit with those harried thoughts that linger
Then, with kind and tender, loving care
She lets them go like November